Verbs in Action
Spring Out

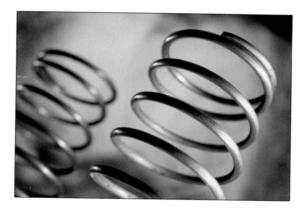

Dana Meachen Rau

Marshall Cavendish
Benchmark
New York

A cat is hiding in the garden.
She sees a mouse.

The cat waits. The mouse does not see her.

4

Then the cat springs! She lands on the mouse. But the mouse gets away.

Spring means to jump out quickly.

Many animals spring out when they are *hunting* for food. A tiger springs out of the jungle to catch a bird.

A *moray eel* springs out of the reef to catch a fish.

Spring also means to jump
again and again. A *kangaroo*
springs across the grasslands
of Australia.

A frog springs through the marsh.

Animals that spring have strong *hind legs*. They help the animals spring fast and far across the ground.

You can spring up and down by jumping.

Jumping on a *trampoline* makes you spring even higher!

13

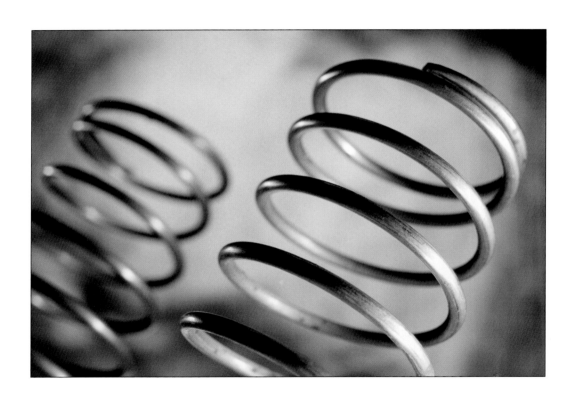

The word "spring" also means a *coiled* piece of wire.

When you push down on a spring, it gets very small. When you let go, it pops back up again.

A spring is what makes a trampoline so bouncy.

Some toys have springs.

Have you ever opened a Jack-in-the-box? Jack springs out of the box to surprise you.

A mattress is filled with springs. Springs make your bed comfortable to sleep on. But a mattress is fun to spring on, too!

The word spring is used in other ways.

You might "spring into action" to clean up your room.

You might want to be the first
one to "spring the news" to your
family that you won an award.

The pipe in your bathroom might "spring a leak" and spill water all over the floor!

Your love of elephants might
"spring from" your visit to the zoo.

Pizza might "spring to mind" when your mother asks what you want for dinner.

There is even a season called spring. Maybe it is called spring because so many new flowers "spring up" from the ground. What a nice surprise!

Challenge Words

coiled (KOYLD)—Wound up into a circle shape.

hind legs (HYND LEGS)—The back legs of an animal.

hunting (HUN-ting)—Catching animals for food.

kangaroo (kang-guh-ROO)—An animal with strong back legs for jumping, small front legs, and a long, powerful tail.

moray eel (mor-AY EEL)—A snake-like fish that lives in warm oceans.

trampoline (tram-puh-LEEN)—A flat piece of material connected by springs to a frame.

Index

Page numbers in **boldface** are illustrations.

With thanks to Nanci Vargus, Ed.D. and Beth Walker Gambro, reading consultants

Marshall Cavendish Benchmark
Marshall Cavendish
99 White Plains Road
Tarrytown, New York 10591-9001
www.marshallcavendish.us

Library of Congress Cataloging-in-Publication Data

Rau, Dana Meachen, 1971–
Spring out / by Dana Meachen Rau.
p. cm. — (Bookworms. Verbs in action)
Includes index.
ISBN 0-7614-1935-7
1. Spring (The English word)—Juvenile literature. 2. English language—Verb—Juvenile literature.
I. Title II. Series: Rau, Dana Meachen, 1971– . Bookworms. Verbs in action.

PE1317.S67R388 2005
428.1—dc22
2004023398

Photo Research by Anne Burns Images

Cover photo: Corbis/Chris Carroll

The photographs in this book are used with permission and through the courtesy of:
Corbis: pp. 1, 4, 14, 26 Royalty Free; p. 2 Roy Morsch; p. 3 Neil Miller; p. 8 Martin Harvey; p. 9 Joe McDonald; p. 10 Raymond Gehman; p. 13 Chris Carroll; p. 17 Bob Krist; p. 21 FK Photo; p. 22 Hutchings Stock Photography; p. 24 LWA-Dann Tardif; p. 29 Charles O'Rear. *SuperStock*: p. 6 Tom Brakefield; p. 7 Frederico Cabello; p. 25 Sadik Demiroz; p. 27 Image Source. *Photri*: p. 18.

Series design by Becky Terhune

Printed in Malaysia
1 3 5 6 4 2